KU-159-066

00232

232

ANT CITIES

Written and illustrated by Arthur Dorros

A & C Black · London

Other books in this series

Dinosaur Bones
Evolution
Feel the Wind
Germs Make Me Sick!
Get Ready for Robots!
Rock Collecting
Snow is Falling
What Makes Day and Night

To Irene Dorros

A CIP catalogue record for this book
is available from the British Library

ISBN 0-7136-3196-1

A & C Black (Publishers) Limited
35 Bedford Row, London WC1R 4JH
This edition © 1989 A & C Black (Publishers) Limited

Published by arrangement with Harper & Row
Publishers Inc., New York
Copyright © 1987 Arthur Dorros

All rights reserved. No part of this publication may be
reproduced, stored in a retrieval system or transmitted
by any means, electronic, mechanical, photocopying,
recording, or otherwise, without prior permission
of A & C Black (Publishers) Limited.

Filmset by August Filmsetting, Haydock, St Helens
Printed in Spain by Salingraf S.A.L.

ANT CITIES

Have you seen ants running busily over a
mound of soil? They may look as if they
are just running around. But ants build
these mounds to live in, and each ant
has work to do.

5

Some ants may disappear into a small hole
in the hill. The hole is the door to their nest.
A nest may have several doors.

The nest is made up of lots of rooms and tunnels.
They were all made by the ants.

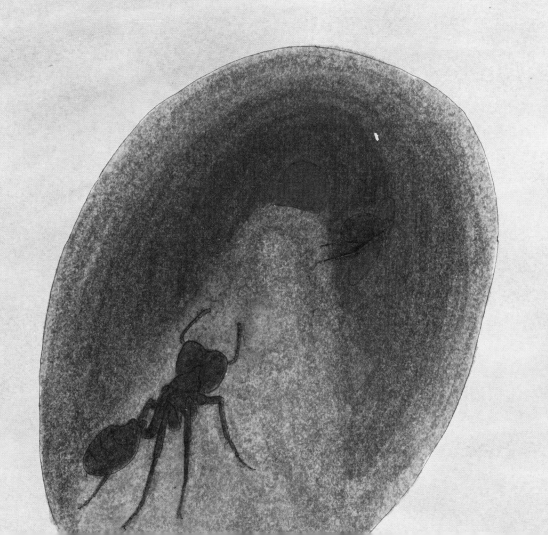

When it is sunny, the top of the nest gets warm.

When it rains, water runs off the hill.

If it gets too wet near the top of the nest, the ants move below.

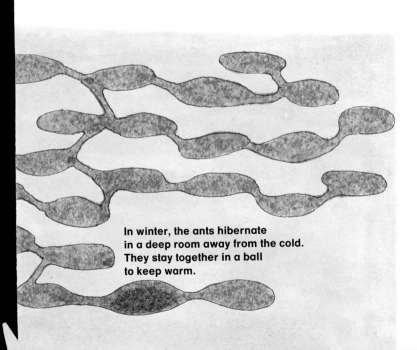

In winter, the ants hibernate in a deep room away from the cold. They stay together in a ball to keep warm.

Underneath the hill, there may be miles of tunnels and hundreds of rooms.

The floors are worn smooth by thousands of tiny feet. It is dark inside the nest. But the ants stay cosy and dry.

9

In the rooms of the nest, worker ants do many different kinds of work. It is like a city; a busy city of ants. Each day, lots of worker ants go out of the city to collect food.

These are harvester ants. They like seeds. They bring lots of them into the city.

A worker ant cracks the husks off the seeds. Another worker will take the husks outside and throw them away.

The ants chew the seeds to make a sort of dough, which they eat or feed to other ants.

Other workers store seeds for the ants to eat later.

Harvester ants often live in hot dry parts of the world.

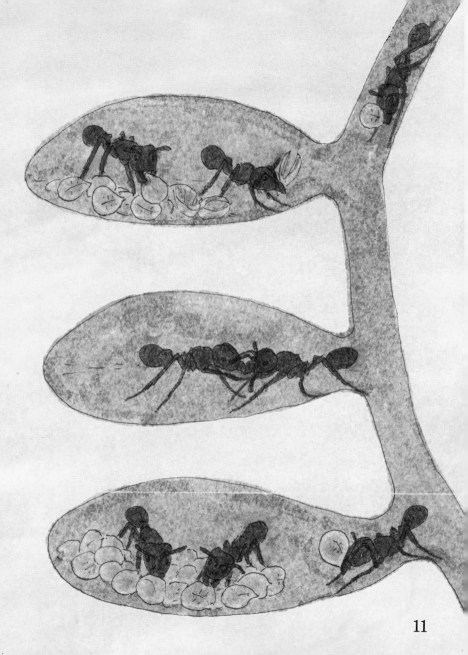

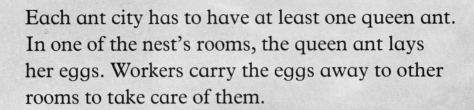

Each ant city has to have at least one queen ant.
In one of the nest's rooms, the queen ant lays
her eggs. Workers carry the eggs away to other
rooms to take care of them.

Without a queen there would be no ant city.
All the other ants in the city grow from the eggs
which the queen lays.

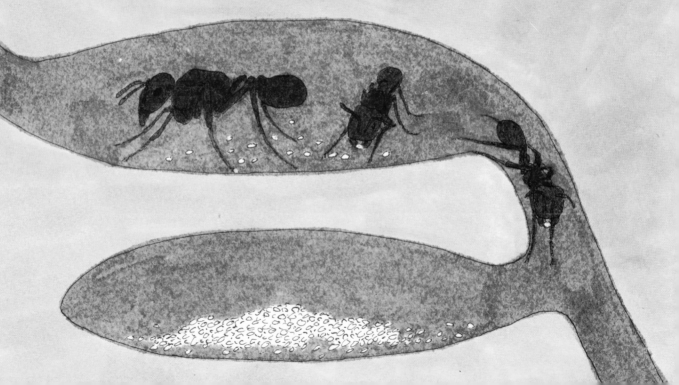

First, the tiny eggs grow into larvae. The worker ants feed the larvae and lick them clean so that they will grow.

Then, the larvae grow into pupae. The workers keep grooming the pupae until they grow into adults.

The queen ant lays thousands and thousands of eggs.
Most of the eggs grow into worker ants. There may
be only one queen ant in an ant city, but there can
be thousands of workers.

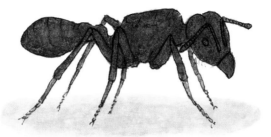

Queen

The queen is usually bigger than the other ants.
She lays eggs that grow into:

Workers

All workers are females.
They do the work in the ant
city. They will also fight to
protect the nest.

New Queens

New queens have wings so
they can fly away
and start new ant cities.
Their wings drop off, and
then the queens lay eggs.

Males

Male ants don't live in
the nest for long.
They fly away with the
new queens to mate.
Then they die.

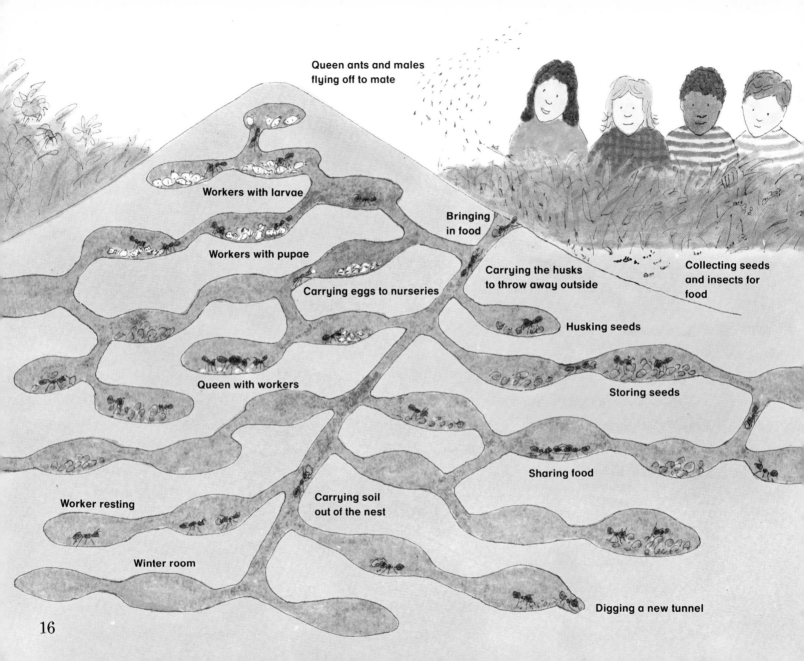

Queen ants and males flying off to mate

Workers with larvae

Workers with pupae

Carrying eggs to nurseries

Bringing in food

Carrying the husks to throw away outside

Collecting seeds and insects for food

Husking seeds

Queen with workers

Storing seeds

Sharing food

Worker resting

Carrying soil out of the nest

Winter room

Digging a new tunnel

16

The queen doesn't tell the workers what to do.
But the workers are busy. Each ant has work
to do. Ants work together to keep the whole
ant city alive.

Workers make the nest bigger by digging new rooms and tunnels. Like tiny dogs, the ants use their feet to dig. Workers pick up pieces of soil in their strong jaws, and carry them outside.

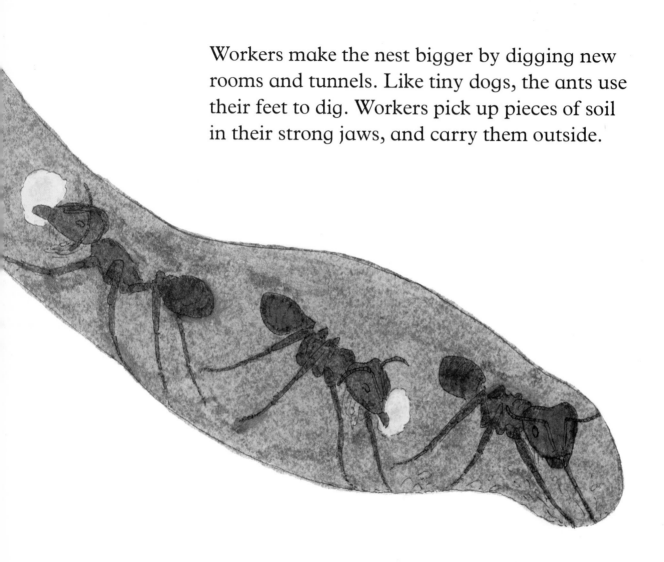

Some ant-hills can be a metre high
and two metres across, though most are smaller.

Ants are great diggers and builders. The ant-hill
is made from the soil which the ants have dug
out of the hill. Imagine all the tiny pieces of
soil it takes to build a hill half a metre high.

19

Outside the ant-hill, the workers look for food. Harvester ants mostly eat seeds, but sometimes they eat insects, too. Many other ants eat insects, and most like sweet things such as honey and fruit.

Ants can bite and sting insects to capture them or to protect themselves. Be careful, because some kinds of ants can bite or sting you, too.

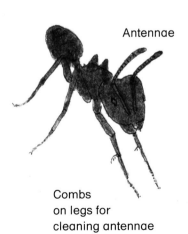

Antennae

Combs
on legs for
cleaning antennae

Ants use their antennae to find food. They touch and smell with their antennae.

Cleaning antennae

Ants 'talk' to each other by touching antennae

21

If one ant finds food, others follow. Soon there will be lots of ants carrying away their lunch.

If one ant can't carry something, others may help. But each worker ant is strong. An ant can lift as much as fifty times its own weight. If people could do that, we could each lift a car.

The workers carry the food back to the ant city.
Ants share the food they find.

Ants eat many foods. But different
kinds of ants like to eat different foods.
There are over 10,000 kinds of ants.

Wood ants mostly eat juices that they suck from the insects they kill.

Meadow ants like to eat the sweet juices, or honeydew, made by aphids. Aphids suck the juices from the plants. Then the ants 'milk' the aphids for honeydew.

Carpenter ants nest in rotting wood. They like sweet juices, which they can get from insects, and from plants, too. They do not live in Britain.

Household ants eat sweets and other food they find in people's houses. They are very small ants.

Leaf-cutting ants, or parasol ants, cut down leaves to make underground gardens. They grow tiny 'mushrooms' in the gardens for food. Leaf-cutting ants are small and live only in tropical America.

Army ants travel in large groups like armies. They devour huge numbers of insects, and other animals. Army ants live only in tropical parts of the world.

The different kinds of ants have found many ways to make their cities, so they can live in many kinds of places.

Janitor ants make their nests in hollowed-out tree twigs. They live in the warmer parts of the world. The soldier janitor ant – a kind of worker ant – has a big, plug-shaped head it can use for a door.

Door to janitor ants' nest

Many kinds of ants make hills or mounds. Maybe you've seen the large mounds of the wood ants in forests. The mounds are often 'thatched' with a layer of dried grass or pine needles.

Wood ant

Pavement ants are tiny – 4 mm long.
Some ants are as big as 5 cm long.

You may have seen black pavement ants. They can live
under pavements and also under paths and stones
in your garden.

Many ants build their nests in rotting wood.

There are small ant cities with just a few ants.
There are big ant cities with many, many ants.
Ants have been found at the tops of the highest
buildings and even on ships at sea.

Ants can make their cities almost anywhere.
Look around and you'll probably find an ant
city, busy with ants.

Make your own 'ant farm' and see how ants live
underground. If you want your farm to last a
long time, make sure that you include a queen ant.

Collecting jar

Remember when
you collect ants to be
very careful. Some
ants can bite or sting.

Fill to about here

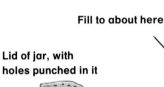

Lid of jar, with
holes punched in it

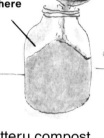

- Sift some woodland soil or garden pottery compost
  into a large jam jar.
- Put a small piece of damp sponge into the jar so that the
  ants have something to drink. Don't pour water into the
  jar because the ants might drown. But don't let the soil
  get too dry because the ants will shrivel up and die.
- Feed the ants regularly, but don't give them too much food
  at a time. Most ants will enjoy a slice of orange and some
  small pieces of raw meat. When you collect the ants, look
  to see what they are eating.
- Now you have an ant farm.
- Keep it in a dark place. When you want to watch the ants,
  take the jar into the light.

Lid with holes

Sponge   Food

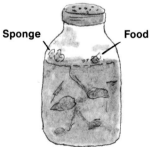

Soil between two
flat pieces of glass
or plastic

Tape   Screen

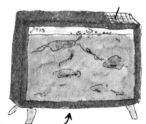

You might want to make or buy a big ant farm like this.